This journal holds
the awesome writings of:

....

you aRe
Amazing!

If you could spend a day inside the setting of any book, which would you choose and why?

Write a rhyming poem describing your bedroom
or the place where you spend the most time.

Think about your favorite sport.
What do you like about it?

Write a short story starting with this sentence:

I'd spent the whole weekend working on my Halloween costume, and it was guaranteed to be the best at the party.

The ALL about ME!

WORD LIST

1. _____   11. _____
2. _____   12. _____
3. _____   13. _____
4. _____   14. _____
5. _____   15. _____
6. _____   16. _____
7. _____   17. _____
8. _____   18. _____
9. _____   19. _____
10. _____   20. _____

Write 20 words (like funny, happy, thoughtful, artistic, etc.) that describe who you are!

Tell the story of a time that something unbelievably funny happened.

Set yourself three goals to accomplish in the next year. What are they? What steps will you take to reach them?

What's one book you didn't like so much?
Now think of one reason why someone
you know should read it . . .

A genie appears and offers you three wishes.
What do you wish for? (No wishing for more wishes!)

Write a short story starting with this sentence:

"Well, this just raises more questions than it answers," Jolie said.

Who is one of your real-life heroes?

Why do you look up to him or her?

Describe the perfect birthday.
What do you do? Who is there?

Describe how modern technology plays a part in your daily routine to someone from 200 years ago.

What do you love? Doodle or write about the things or activites you enjoy most.

Design your own superhero.

What powers does he or she have?

Write a short story starting with this sentence:
Looking back on it, perhaps I was just in
the right place at the right time.

Describe a step-by-step process for how
to do something you're good at.

What is your best habit? How did you develop it?

Give someone directions to the library without drawing a map.

You've begun to suspect that your house is haunted. What's been happening?

Write a short story starting with this sentence:
It's not like I would have purchased a cursed hamster on purpose.

Describe your style.

Share 5 special things about yourself
that make you who you are!

When you're in a bad mood, how do
you make yourself feel better?

Your principal announces that nominations are open for this year's Teacher of the Year award. Explain why your favorite teacher should get the award.

Cut an advertisement out of a magazine or newspaper and paste it in here. Read it closely. How is it trying to sell you its product?

Write a letter of thanks to your favorite teacher.

Write words to a new lullaby. Make it rhyme!

List 10 things that you are grateful for. They can be big or small, objects or people or even concepts.

What are the top 5 songs on your current life soundtrack? If you had to cut one, which one would you cut? Why?

What book do you think everyone should read? Why?

What makes you happy? Doodle or write about something
that makes you smile in the starburst.

Write a short story starting with this sentence:
My mother was mad about the broken vase,
that much was certain.

Compare and contrast your two favorite fictional characters.

What is a habit you would like to develop?

How can you get started on it?

How can you motivate yourself to keep going?

Your best friend wants to go bowling this Saturday, but you want to go to the beach instead. Convince your friend to join you.

Cut a picture of a person out of a magazine and paste or tape it to this page. Make up a name and a backstory for this person.

Write a short story starting with this sentence:
The night Stef accidentally joined a beauty pageant,
it was raining pretty hard.

Pick a fairy tale, such as Little Red Riding Hood or Cinderella, that you know well. Many of these tales are hundreds of years old and were originally told to children to teach lessons. What lessons does your fairy tale teach?

When and/or where do you get the most done?
What is it about that time and/or space
that helps you feel productive?

Dream big! Write or doodle about something you
intend to accomplish in the bubble.

Tape something flat to this page. Now describe it in words, using as much detail as you can.

Describe a book you've read, using *at least* 250 words. Now describe it again, using *no more than* 100 words.

Write a short story starting with this sentence:
My first day on the job at the aquarium
started with a bang.

Write a rhyming birthday message for a friend.

Tell the story of a time you overcame a challenge.
How did you do it? How did it feel?

What's more important, money or love? Why?

Press a leaf or flower in between these pages until it is flat and dried. As you do so, think about seasons. Which season is your favorite? Why?

Write a short story starting with this sentence: Gordon wouldn't normally have spoken to Darla outside of science class, but she was the only one who might be able to break the code.

Be flattered! Write the best compliment you've ever received (or write
one that you'd like to receive!) And don't forget to say "Thank you!"

Arrange a piece of ribbon into a design on this page, and glue it down. (Or use colorful tape if you like.) Write a poem using the space around or inside it.

What does your weekly schedule look like?
Describe a typical week in your life.

Who is the bravest person you know? Why?

What is one thing you admire about each of your three best friends? It can be different for each!

Write a short story starting with this sentence:

Reya's dog was her best friend.

Paste an empty wrapper on this page. Now describe it in words, using as much detail as you can.

Describe something that never fails to make you happy.

How long should a school day be? Why?

Be proud! Doodle or write about your qualities or accomplishments that you are most proud of.

Spend 20 minutes reading something really unexpected—something you would normally never pick up. Use this space to respond to it.

Write a short story starting with this sentence:

The lady in purple drew herself up to her full height.

What is your ideal breakfast?

What is one good habit you developed on purpose?
What was that process like?

Compare and contrast soccer and basketball.

Cut letters out of a magazine and paste them to this page, spelling out your name. What does your name mean? Is it fitting for your personality?

Write a short story starting with this sentence: The cave in front of me was clearly someone's hideaway.

Talk about one of the accomplishments that you're the proudest of. How did you pull it off?

How would five of your closest friends or
family members describe you?

Create social media profiles written in the voice of 3 fictional characters of your choice.
Don't forget a villain!

Rewrite the fairy tale of your choice from the perspective of the villain.

Compare and contrast childhood and adulthood.